How do you say "Happy

Thanksgiving" to a Scotsman?

Much love,

Earl and Adalynne

CHRISTIAN HESKETH

TARTANS

OCTOPUS BOOKS

London · New York · Sydney · Hong Kong

ACKNOWLEDGMENTS

The author acknowledges the great debt she owes to Mr R. Hutcheson and Mr B. Skinner, of the Scottish National Portrait Gallery; to Mr A. Haswell Miller; Mr W. Thorburn of the Scottish United Services Museum; Major David Murray of the Queen's Own Cameron Highlanders; and Sir Iain Moncrieff of that Ilk Bart. The following illustrations are reproduced by gracious permission of Her Majesty the Queen from the Royal Collection at Windsor Castle, figures 20, 36.

The author and publishers also wish to thank the following owners for kind permission to reproduce pictures in their private collections: The Duke of Atholl, figures 59, 108; The Duke of Buccleuch, figures 89, 93; The Duke of Richmond and Gordon, figure 86; The Duke of Roxburghe, figure 43; The Earl of Home, figure 39; The Earl of Moray, figures 88, 92; The Countess of Seafield, figures 8, 9, 52; The Earl of Wemyss, figure 23; Lord Lovat, figure 117; Lord Macdonald, figure 48; Lord David Stuart, figure 49; The Hon. Hugh Fraser, figure 90; Sir Ian Forbes Leith òf Fyvie, figure 53; Sir Gregor MacGregor of MacGregor, figure 61; Dame Flora MacLeod of MacLeod, figure 45; Sir David Ogilvy Bt, figure 32; Ninian Brodie of Brodie Esq., figures 91, 107; N. Cameron Esq., figure 98; Mrs Dalyell of the Binns, figure 82; the Marquis of Bute, figure 18; A. Haswell Miller Esq., figure 4 and title page; Victor Malcolm Esq., figure 112; Anthony Murray of Dollerie Esq., figures 33, 38; Mr and Mrs Mark S. Murray Threipland, figure 51; Mrs Skeoch Cumming, figure 87. The author and publishers are also grateful to the Commanding Officer of the Black Watch for permission to reproduce figure 114, and to the Commanding Officer, Queen's Own Cameron Highlanders, for figures 109 and 113.

Figures 31, 69 appear by courtesy of the Royal Company of Archers; figures 7, 68, 70, 96, 97, 100, 102, 111, 116 by courtesy of Messrs Scott Adie, Tartan Warehouse, London; and figure 84 by courtesy of John Dewar and Sons Ltd, Distillers.

The following illustrations are reproduced by courtesy of the Scottish National Portrait Gallery and the Scottish United Services Museum; 2, 14, 16, 17, 19, 21, 22, 23, 26, 29, 30, 32, 34, 39, 40, 41, 44, 46, 52, 54, 55, 56, 57, 58, 63, 67, 71, 73, 74, 76, 77, 78, 81, 82, 83, 85, 86, 87, 91, 93, 98, 103, 107.

Figures 1, 12, 13 are reproduced by permission of the British Museum; figure 5 by permission of the National Museum of Ireland; figure 10 by permission of the Bodleian Library, Oxford; and figure 24 by permission of the Inverness Town Council.

Figure 118 appears by courtesy of the Trustees of the Tate Gallery.

Figure 48 appears by permission of *Country Life* Ltd; figure 45 by permission of the Medici Society; and figure 110 by permission of *The Scotsman*.

The tartans for figures 35, 99, 105 were supplied by William Anderson and Sons, Kiltmakers, Edinburgh.

Figures 17, 32, 56 are by Messrs Annans, Glasgow; figures 94, 95 by the Radio Times Hulton Picture Library; figure 3 by J. L. Rodger ARPS, Stornoway; figures 50, 62, 65, 66, 72, 79 by John R. Freeman and Co, from the British Museum; and figures 15, 28, 49, 104, 118 by Ian Graham. All other photographs were specially taken by Tom Scott, Edinburgh, from private collections, the Scottish United Services Museum and the Scottish National Portrait Gallery.

This edition first published 1972 by
OCTOPUS BOOKS LIMITED
59 Grosvenor Street, London W.1

ISBN 7064 0033 X

PRODUCED BY MANDARIN PUBLISHERS LIMITED AND PRINTED IN HONG KONG

Preceding page
Four impressions of Highland dress

Early History of Tartan

1 This drawing in the Ghent Library is one of the earliest pictures of a Highlander in native dress. It was made in 1570

IN WRITING ABOUT TARTAN, it is necessary to make it clear from the outset, that although the subject is by no means new, even now it continues to provoke a large measure of disagreement among its more articulate devotees. Thus, while one school of thought maintains that the individual patterns, or 'setts' as they are called, of the numerous clan tartans on sale today are as old as the clan system itself, another holds, with equal tenacity, to the belief that all so-called family tartans are the invention of the nineteenth or at the very earliest of the eighteenth century. It is both easy and tempting to say that somewhere between these two extremes the truth must lie, but this statement in itself would be an over-simplification.

There is plenty of evidence to suggest that many of the best known Scottish tartans now in existence (among which are some misleadingly labelled ancient) are no more than tailors' tartans that owe their origin to some astute manufacturer in the reign of Queen Victoria. But, and here is the rub, it can also be proved that certain clans did achieve a kind of uniformity in tartan design at a much earlier date. If it is difficult to ascertain when tartans were first invented, it is no easier to discover how they were worn. For the little kilt or *philabeg*, to give it its older, Gaelic name, now universally acepted as the standard dress for Highlanders and pseudo-Highlanders everywhere, is in itself of comparatively modern origin and derives in turn from that much older and now obsolete garment, the belted plaid [figure 17]. But let us begin at the beginning.

The word tartan is derived from the French *tartaine*, a name that was given originally to a certain kind of material regardless of its colour. It was only at a later date, when all Highland tartan grew to be chequered, that it acquired its more specialized modern meaning. The Gaelic word for tartan was *breacan*, meaning parti-

2 A Highland chief, possibly Lord Breadalbane, by Michael Wright, *c.* 1660

3 There was a similarity between Irish and Scottish dress before the sixteenth century. The Macleod tombstone, Eye church, Isle of Lewis

coloured or speckled. Every tartan in use today represents a different arrangement of colours, stripes and checks, and each individual pattern, or 'sett', to use the more technical term, goes by the name of the clan, family, or regiment with which it is associated. Although the kilt is the most popular of all tartan garments, plaids and trews are also worn, and tartan skirts in the case of the women.

The first written reference to Highland dress occurs in the *Saga of Magnus Barefoot* in 1093, where it is stated that when the king returned from an expedition to the

4 In order to put on a belted plaid, a rectangular piece of material roughly 16 feet long and 5 feet wide, the wearer laid the plaid on the ground with his belt beneath it. He then pleated the material over the belt and lay down on top of it with the bottom at knee level. He belted the material round his waist and stood up, leaving the long unpleated tail to fall behind. He then put on his coat, waistcoat and sporran. For normal use the tail was looped on the left shoulder and tucked in, or the whole of it could be used as a cloak

5 The Burke effigy at Glinsk, Co. Galway, wears the same garments as the Highlander from Islay (*opposite*)

west, he adopted the costume of the western lands, and thereafter went about barelegged 'having a short tunic and also upper garments'. Attempts have been made, from time to time, to claim this short tunic as the first kilt, but it seems clear that Magnus in fact wore the *leine croich* or saffron shirt common to both the Irish and the Scots at that time. It was still in vogue in the Highlands some five centuries later when John Major wrote an account of the wild Scots. 'From the middle of the thigh to the foot', he observed, 'they have no covering for the leg, clothing themselves with a mantle instead of an upper garment, and a shirt dyed with saffron... The common people of the Highland Scots rush into battle having their body clothed with a linen garment manifoldly sewed and painted or daubed with pitch, with a covering of deerskin.' The similarity that existed at this time between the Highland tunic and the saffron shirt worn by the Irish can be traced on many of the grave slabs scattered over Ireland and the Western Isles [figures 3, 5, 6]. Although the Scottish version of the *teine croich* seems always to have been dyed a single colour, in Ireland a more elaborate system prevailed, by which the stripes on a man's clothing were clear indications of his rank. Thus the *Ard Righ*, or High King, was entitled to seven, of which one was purple; the *Oblambs*, or learned men, had six, and so on, down to the kerns who had to be content with stripes of one colour only. It is curious to find an unconscious echo of the hierarchical stripes of fifteenth century Ireland in the portrait of Donald Grant of Glenbeg painted three centuries later.

At the end of the fifteenth century the Lordship of the Isles was finally forfeited to the Crown, and from then on the Kings of Scotland, anxious to substitute a more personal authority for the uneasy suzerainty they had exercised before, began to pay increasingly frequent visits to the northern parts of their kingdom. In 1538 James V ordered himself the first Highland suit ever worn by a member of the Royal family, for which the modest account, laboriously entered by the Lord High Treasurer of the day, is still extant: two and a quarter ells of 'variant cullorit velvit' to be 'ane schort Heland coit' at £ 6 the ell: £ 13.10; three ells of 'Heland tartane to be hoiss' (hose) at 4s 4d the ell: 13s. What the king wore was a short multi-coloured jacket and a pair of tartan trews, a form of dress that is at least as old, if not older than the belted plaid. It can be seen

6 A Highland grave slab in Islay

in the later stage of its development at its elegant best in the portraits by Allan Ramsay of Norman, twenty-second Chief of Macleod, at Dunvegan [figure 45] and of the third Duke of Perth [figure 43]. Not all the king's subjects, unfortunately, were so neatly attired: 'They wear no clothes,' wrote an astonished French visitor in 1556, 'except their dyed shirts and a light woolen rug of several colours'.

One of the most surprising features in all the early accounts of Highland dress is the apparent inadequacy of the clothes worn [figure 1]. It is hard to see how anyone, clad only in a shirt and a rug, could have long survived the rigours of a Highland winter, and the water-resisting qualities of linen shirts, even when daubed with pitch, must have been severely tested by the remorseless rains of the Outer Hebrides. Without a doubt the two main reasons to which this scantiness of attire is attributable were, in the first place poverty, and in the second a shortage of wool. It has already been pointed out by many previous writers that the sheep, now so familiar a feature of the Highland scene, is by no means an indigenous one, and it is not without significance that the word hardly exists among Highland place names. In Ross and Cromarty, for instance, not a single Gaelic name and only two Norse ones derive from it. It follows that at the time when tartans first began to assume a definite pattern, the material out of which they were made was both expensive and scarce. Until the nineteenth century, it was the custom for the women of the house to weave whatever tartan was required by their families, and they used for this purpose a hand-loom of which the shuttle was thrown from hand to hand. The width of the material, for this reason, was never more than thirty inches, and in order to produce a belted plaid it was necessary to sew two lengths of tartan together. The finished garment was no more than a rectangular length of cloth, some fifteen feet long by five feet wide, that could be adapted without difficulty to suit the individual needs of the wearer. At night he slept in it, and by day it served as a kilt and plaid combined [figure 4]. Later, when the clan setts became standardized, the weavers made use of pattern sticks to record the design of particular tartans. The proper number of threads for each line or check of the pattern was wound round the stick in the correct order, and the stick itself handed down religiously from one generation to the next.

7

7 A modern dirk for dress occasions

8 The Piper to the Laird of Grant, painted by Richard Waitt in 1714. The Piper's tartan is similar to that of the Champion

9 Alastair Grant Mohr, honorary Champion to the Laird of Grant, also painted by Richard Waitt

Le capitaine sauuage.

Vous pourrez voir icier Les Escossoys,
Tel capitaine faisant là Leur scienie,
Qui souuent sont nuysance auy Anglois,
Peu de profit Leur fait faire maints tours.

La sauuage d'escosse.

Si tu mets L'œil dessus ceste figure,
A ceste fin que cettain tu ey sore,
C'est La sauuage au pays Escossoys,
Qc peaux dessue encontre La froidure.

10 A Highland lady and gentleman in 1562, from an old French book. The Irish gentry wore much the same cloaks and furs as these

By the end of the sixteenth century the saffron shirt was on its way out, largely, it is said, because the Elizabethan conquest of Ireland put an end to the export of linen from that country. But that shirts of a kind were still being worn at least as late as the Civil War (1644-5) is proved by the orders issued at the battle of Kilsyth, by the King's Lieutenant, the Marquis of Montrose. On that hot August day, he commanded his Highland levies to lay aside their heavy plaids, and knot the long tails of their shirts between their legs.

11 The supporters of the arms of Skene of that ilk, taken from a store at Skene in 1672, wear very elaborate Highland dress. The figure on the left has trews and a plaid. From Nisbet's *Heraldic Plates*

12 This child, from Gordon's Map of Aberdeen, 1661, is sometimes thought to be wearing a very early example of the modern kilt

With the eclipse of the saffron shirt, any lingering resemblance between early Highland and Irish dress finally disappeared, and from then on tartan began to assume a character entirely of its own. Purple and blue seem to have been the colours most favoured by the early wearers, but brown was popular too, perhaps as a camouflage. An early picture shows one of the Earls of Moray wearing a tartan in two shades of brown only.

So far there is no indication that any of these early tartans were looked upon as the exclusive property of the individual clans, but it is more than likely that over a period of time the setts associated with particular districts came to be called by the name of the clan most prominent in the area. This is what appears to have happened in Islay, where, from 1587 onwards, the annual ground rent, payable to the Crown, consisted of sixty ells of black, white and green cloth. Now the lands in question belonged during that time, except for one brief period, to the Macleans, and it cannot be entirely coincidental that to this day the Maclean tartan is made up of the same three colours [figure 99]. But, alas for the theorist, this admirable consistency is rare indeed, and more often than not one looks in vain for even the most tenuous connection between the tartans worn by famous Highland figures of the past and their fellow clansmen today.

Although it is only very recently that the Highlands have come into fashion as a holiday resort (Dr Johnson, it will be remembered, was appalled by the desolation of the country) there were, at all times, a few intrepid travellers who took an interest in the country and the customs of the people. Such a one was John Taylor, the self-styled Water Poet, who, in 1618 paid a visit to Braemar, and has left an account of all that he saw there. In August and September of every year, he noted, the nobility and gentry of the whole kingdom visited the Highlands in great numbers for the sport. All strangers were expected to wear Highland dress, and had they omitted to do so, it would have been considered deliberately insulting by their hosts, and, in return, neither dogs nor game would have been forthcoming. Taylor himself conformed to the local custom, and what he has to say about Highland dress is all the more interesting coming, as it does, from one who had himself worn the clothes he so minutely describes. 'The Highland men', he observed, 'for the most part speak nothing but Irish and in former times were those people who were called the Red Shankes. Their habit is shoes with but one sole apiece; stockings (which they call short hose) made of a warm stuff of divers colours, which they call tartan. As for breeches, many of them, nor their forefathers, never wore any, but a jerkin of the same stuff that their hose is of, their garters being bands of wreaths of hay or straw, with a plaid about their shoulders, which is a mantle of divers colours, much finer and lighter stuff than their hose, with blue caps on their heads, a handkerchief knit with two knots about their necks; and thus they are attired.' The Scottish mercenaries of Mackay's regiment who fought under Gustavus Adolphus a few years later wore clothes very similar to these, but with the addition of gold chains round their necks [figure 13]. These they carried as a portable form of ransom, and in order to secure good treatment for themselves, in case

13 A very early picture of Highland dress; these Scottish mercenary soldiers of the Thirty Years' War, possibly from Mackay's Regiment, wear bonnets and tartan

In solchem Habit Gehen die 800 In Stettin angekommen Irrländer oder Irren.

G. Keler Ex.

Es ist ein Starckes dauerhafftigs Volck behilfft sich mit geringer speiß hatt es nicht brodt so Essen sie Würtzeln, Wans auch die Notturfft erfordert Können sie des Tages Uber die 20 Teütscher meilweges lauffen, haben neben Musqueden Ihre Bogen vnd Köcher vnd Lange Messer.

14 A Sergeant in a belted plaid, from a drawing of a Highland Regiment on the march in Flanders, 1743

they were wounded. Perhaps the most interesting point that emerges from Taylor's narrative is that in his day the wearing of tartan and Highland dress in general was not confined exclusively to chiefs and their clansmen.

It is often said that until a glow of post-Jacobite sentiment and the novels of Sir Walter Scott made the assumption of tartan respectable, no one but a Highlander would have dreamt of wearing it. This point of view was forcibly expressed by the Lowland laird who in answer to the question: 'Does your family have a tartan?' replied with spirit, 'No, thank God. My ancestors were always able to afford trousers'. But among many of the great families whose lands lay on both sides of what is loosely called the Highland Line, this mythical barrier was never so rigidly defined as some modern writers would have us believe. The Drummonds, the Grahams, the Ogilvys, to name only a few, were none of them of Highland stock, but many of their tenants were, and they themselves undoubtedly wore Highland dress whenever the occasion demanded it, and in many cases understood, if they did not also speak, the Gaelic language. The same thing applies in Aberdeenshire, where the Huntlys, as successive heads of the great house of Gordon, unquestionably played the part of Highland magnates, though they were not, strictly speaking, clan chiefs. One has only to read the names of the officers who fought on the Jacobite side in the '15 and the '45 to realize how artificial is the distinction continually being made between Highland and Lowland. The portrait of James Moray of Abercairney, painted in 1745, is an indication of how fine the dividing line between the two could be, for though the Morays were of predominantly Lowland descent, his dress is that of a Highland gentleman [figure 34]. Paradoxically enough, not all Highlanders chose to be painted in tartan. Hogarth's famous picture of the fifteenth Lord Lovat, painted only a year later than the Abercairney portrait, shows a clan chief arrayed in the conventional English clothes of the period. Nor is this an isolated example. The Earls of Argyll were painted on numerous occasions during the seventeenth century, but never in Highland dress. The first chief of Clan Campbell to be painted in tartan was the second Duke of Argyll in 1789.

15 A woman of clan Urquhart. A fanciful nineteenth-century reconstruction from McIan's *The Costumes of the Clans*, 1857

16 Sir Robert
Dalrymple of
Castleton, one
of the earliest
pictures of a
Lowland laird
wearing tartan
Anon. *c.* 1720

This does not mean that the chiefs despised the clothes worn by their own clansmen, or regarded them in the light of fancy dress, but it is an indication that before the '45 Highlanders were not dressed exclusively in tartan, a fact that the nineteenth century has done something to obscure.

By the time James VI of Scotland succeeded to the English throne it is likely that a number of district tartans were already in existence, some of which may well be the prototypes of clan tartans actually in use today. This claim cannot, however, be made for most of the early designs, which were no more than the creation of individual weavers, with no tribal significance whatever. The first occasion on which a conscious effort was made to enforce uniformity throughout a whole clan was in 1618, when Sir Robert Gordon of Gordonstoun, then Tutor of Sutherland, wrote to Murray of Pulrossie, 'requesting him to furl his pennon when the Earl of Sutherland's banner was displayed, and to remove the red and white lines from the plaids of his men so as to bring their dress into harmony with that of the other septs'. As the original of this letter cannot now be found, it is open to the sceptic to say that, like Ossian, it may never have existed, but what cannot be denied is that Sir Robert, who was an energetic man with a passion for order, did write other letters in much the same style. So the forgery, if forgery it be, is a good one. With the outbreak of the Civil War the clans found themselves involved in a struggle of which the origins were to most of them obscure. Some were drawn into the ranks of the Covenanting army, and took part in the invasion of England where their 'antique' appearance attracted the contemptuous notice of Defoe. 'Their swords were extravagantly, and I think insignificantly long... These fellows looked when drawn out like a regiment of Merry-Andrews ready for Bartholomew Fair.' According to another eye-witness most of the men still carried bows and arrows and were dressed in 'a pair of bases of plaid and stockings of the same... a mantle of plaid cast over left shoulder, and under the right arm'.

17 (*far left*) Lord Duffus, painted by the English artist Richard Waitt c. 1710, wears a belted plaid

18 (*left*) Unlike the majority of their clansmen, the chiefs usually rode, and therefore often wore the more convenient riding dress of trews and a plaid; the second Earl of Breadalbane as a boy, a portrait attributed to Kneller

19 Lord Glenorchy by Sir Godfrey Kneller

20 George III as a child in Archers' uniform by Du Pan. This is the first time that a Hanoverian prince appears in tartan

21 This reasonably authentic picture of female costume in the early eighteenth century probably shows the white *airsaids* described by Martin Martin, the Laird of MacLeod's agent

22 A Highlander in a belted plaid and trews, a dress often described, from a print by Jaques Basire

If 'a pair of bases' means a petticoat, as is sometimes claimed, then here we have the earliest known reference to the kilt as a garment on its own, separate and distinct from the plaid. There is an objection to this however, for the disputed words could equally well be intended as a description of trews, which are known to have been in common use at the time. Besides, if the kilt was already known before the middle of the seventeenth century, it seems extraordinary that a garment so practical should not have come into general use until nearly a hundred years later. The only other piece of evidence that supports the theory of an earlier origin is the small figure of the kneeling boy in Gordon's Map of Aberdeen [figure 12].

The Civil War represents a turning point in Highland history, for it marks the beginning of that close connection with the house of Stewart which was to be the glory and ruin of the clans. This, in its turn, had an incalculable influence on the development of tartan, for it was through Jacobitism, and the romantic feelings to which the movement gave rise, that an enthusiasm for all things Highland first spread to the polite world. None of this however, could have been foreseen in 1644, when the appearance presented by the King's Highland army was to most Scots as outlandish as it was horrifying. From the savage campaign that followed have sprung stories and legends without number, some of which are remembered to this day. The white spats of the Highland regiments are said to be a perpetual reminder of the winter march to Inverlochy in 1645, when the clansmen wrapped the torn remains of their shirts round their legs and feet, to protect them from the February snows. In order to survive at all under such conditions, we are told, they used to soak their plaids in cold water before sleeping in them, so that the heat of their bodies would produce a warm vapour from the damp cloth, and when the Catholics in the army gathered to hear Mass, those same plaids were stretched behind the makeshift altars to shield them from the wind and rain. Throughout the campaign the King's general, Montrose, fared no better than his men, and on one occasion, at least, he too wore Highland dress. Whether this took the form of trews or the belted plaid is not recorded, but it is probable that like Charles Edward at a later date, he wore the clothes in which a man might most easily ride, *i.e.* trews. Cleland, who wrote a satirical poem some thirty years later, describing the appearance

23 Allan Ramsay's portrait of Francis, seventh Earl of Wemyss and his wife Catherine, is somewhat similar to his portrait of Norman, twenty-second chief of Macleod; both the sitters wear what is now known as Rob Roy tartan

of the Highland host, found that the chief commanders and standard-bearers wore trews with plaids and were mounted, while the rank and file marched on foot and had little else besides their skins to cover them:

> Their head, their neck, their legs and thighs
> Are influenced by the skies.
> Without a clout to interrupt them
> They need not strip them when they whip them.

Descriptions of female attire are far less common, but we do know that from an early date the plaid was worn equally by both sexes: 'the womens' colours much more lively, and the squares larger than the mens'... This serves them for a veil and covers both head and body'. Sometimes the material used was silk. At the same time the use of tartan was not confined entirely to clothes, for the Invernahyle Bible shows that it could also, on occasion, be used as a binding for books.

In 1688 the Jacobite clans rose again in support of the now exiled Stuarts, and after the pyrrhic victory of Killicrankie in which their commander was killed, the Jacobite standard-bearer conceived the ambitious notion of writing another *Aeneid*, in which the brief glories of the campaign should receive due recognition. The result was the *Grameid*, a work in which faint echoes of Virgil are almost obliterated by the sounds of Highland warfare. In it we read of the clans drawn up in saffron array, of Glengarry's men in scarlet hose and plaids crossed with a purple stripe, and Lochiel in a coat of three colours. The plaid worn by MacNeill of Barra 'rivalled the rainbow' and the Macleod contingent from the Outer Isles wore tunics of ox-hide and were armed somewhat surprisingly with axes, and quivers filled with javelins. None of the descriptions of tartans tally in any way with the setts worn in modern times by the same clans, but they do show, if the poet is to be believed, that at the time he was writing a recognizable pattern of some kind existed, and that this extended to the weapons carried by the different clans, and the badges they wore in their bonnets, as well as to their tartans. In spite of the many fanciful exaggerations to be found in it, the *Grameid* does also embody many curious details not to be met with in any other work. And although it was written half a century before the '45, the clansmen whose deeds it celebrates were to remain virtually unchanged until the last great Jacobite defeat at Culloden put an end to the clan system for ever.

24 This portrait of Major Fraser of Castleleathers by an unknown artist is interesting because it shows trews worn with a sporran of the same material

Before the '45 Rising

25 Helen Balfour, wife of Gavin Hamilton, who was painted by William Mosman in 1742, wears the tartan screen or shawl popular in the eighteenth century

UNTIL THE BEGINNING of the eighteenth century the Highlands stood a little apart from the rest of Scotland, though the extent to which this was true has sometimes been exaggerated, as we have seen. It is, however, undeniable that the sense of isolation engendered by the survival of feudalism, a separate language and the different form of dress, was keenly felt and did not finally disappear till many years later. Communications presented

26 A Scottish rifleman on the march, from a drawing of a Highland Regiment in Flanders, 1743

another problem, for until Marshal Wade created a new system of roads and bridges where before there had been only fords and drovers' tracks, travel in the north was severely restricted—another reason why the country was for long so little known. In one sense, it was the fall of the Stewarts that finally opened up the Highlands, for after 1688 the spread of Jacobitism, a movement supported by at least half of the clans, first drove the administration in Edinburgh and then the government in London to take an active interest in the obscurities of Highland politics. In 1707 the Act of Union took place, a measure so universally disliked in Scotland that it succeeded in uniting all shades of political opinion, temporarily at least, in a common cause. Tartan, hitherto mildly suspect in ruling circles as the garb of brigands and Jacobites, came into its own as the symbol of an outraged nationalism, and from that moment its popularity began to extend far beyond the Highlands. Sir Walter Scott has often been accused of 'tartanising' the Lowlands, and it is certainly true that his influence in this direction was far-reaching. But that the idea did not originate with him is made clear by his own words. 'The general proposition that Lowlanders ever wore plaids is difficult to swallow', he remarked, and added, 'I have been told, and believed until now, that the use of tartans was never general in Scotland (Lowland), until the Union, with the detestation of that measure, led it to be adopted as the National colour, and the ladies all affected tartan screens' [figure 39]. In 1713 the Royal Company of Archers, the Queen's Bodyguard in Scotland, adopted tartan as their uniform, though whether they did so as a gesture of anti-Union feeling, or because so many of the members were Jacobites, it is difficult to say. In the *Caledonian Mercury* of the day, the dress was described as 'antique Roman', a flight of fancy that is in no way supported by the portrait still in existence of James, Earl of Wemyss, in the uniform of Captain-General [figure 31]. Incidentally, the clothes he wore on that occasion remain to this day in the possession of his descendants. The Archers continued to dress in tartan until well into the nineteenth century when it was suddenly decided that the 'antique Roman' garb was not Highland after all, and would no longer do. A change was accordingly made to Lincoln green and this is the colour that has been worn ever since.

As the Highlands grew more accessible to the ordinary

traveller, there was a quickening of interest in the manners and customs obtaining there, and from the accounts that survive a picture emerges of the kind of life that was being led in the north at the beginning of the eighteenth century. As far as dress was concerned, there had been no major change since the plaid had ousted the saffron shirt a hundred years before, but clan tartans, those hitherto shadowy things, were beginning to take definite shape. Martin Martin, a native of Skye and the Laird of Macleod's agent, was the first person to observe 'that every Isle differs from each other in their fancy of making Plaids, as to the stripes in breadth and colours'. The same was true, he thought, of other parts of the Highlands, where the sett of a man's tartan revealed his place of origin. Unfortunately Martin did not specify what happened in the case of islands occupied by more than one clan. Skye, for instance, contained both Macdonalds and Macleods. Did these age-old rivals wear their own distinctive setts, or did they share a common district tartan out of which clan tartans ultimately developed? On this point he is silent, though he did observe that a great deal of ingenuity was practised in sorting the colours, 'so as to be agreeable to the nicest fancy', an indication that in his day the taste of the individual was still a major factor in tartan design. To the same source we are indebted for a description of the women. They wore white plaids, called *Airsaids*, striped in black, blue and red. These garments, which reached from the neck to the feet, were fastened on the breast with a silver buckle [figure 21]. Underneath it the sleeves were of scarlet cloth, trimmed with gold lace, and on their heads they wore tightly banded linen kerchiefs. Alas, there are no absolutely authentic surviving pictures to show how the Highland ladies looked in all their finery.

At about the time when Martin was compiling his careful note, on the other side of Scotland the chiefs of the clan Grant were making a determined attempt to standardize the tartan of their men. Six hundred of them were given orders to don tartan coats, all of which had to be of one colour and cut. Shortly after, Sir Ludovic Grant issued a further command, that all tenants must, by a certain date, provide themselves with Highland coats, trews, and short hose of red and green tartan 'set broad-springed'. His son Alexander went even further, and stipulated that in addition to the red and green tartan, all the gentlemen and commons of his name must wear whiskers. These instruc-

27 Corporal Malcolm McPherson of the Black Watch, who was shot in the Tower of London for mutiny in 1743

tions do not seem to have elicited an immediate response, for among the Castle Grant collection of pictures there are nearly a dozen family portraits, all painted in Sir Alexander's lifetime, and all by the same artist, the itinerant Englishman Richard Waitt. In none of them do the whiskers nor the broad-springed sett appear. One is the picture of Donald Grant, mentioned earlier, in which the pattern of the plaid is made up, not of the usual checks and lines, but of different coloured stripes only. Out of all the Grant pictures only two, the Piper and the Champion, can be said to display either the same tartan or one that in any way resembles the clan sett in use today [figures 8, 9]. One conclusion that could be drawn from this is that the idea of a standardized tartan had so little appeal that the Grant chiefs found it easier to impose on their own personal attendants than on the gentlemen of the clan. In another passage, the tartan is described as 'red and green dyce', which may have been a version of

28 A woman in MacNicol tartan, from MacIan's *Costumes of the Clans*

29 A Highland costume of trews, plaid and coat, acquired by Sir John Hynde in 1744, three years before the Dress Act made the wearing of tartan illegal

30 A Highland lady's marriage costume of the mid-eighteenth century

31 James, fifth Earl of Wemyss, in Archers'
uniform, by an unknown artist, *c.* 1715. The
Royal Company of Archers, who are the
Queen's bodyguard in Scotland, were the
first organised body to adopt tartan as a
uniform

the black and red Rob Roy. This sett, now regarded as
the personal tartan of the MacGregor chiefs and their
family, was then looked upon in a somewhat different
light, and worn with equal freedom by Lord Ogilvy in
Angus, and a Macleod chieftain in Skye [figures 32 and
45].

After the Rising of 1715 it became apparent to King
George's government that if a curb were not put upon the
activities of the Jacobite clans, there would be worse
trouble to follow. To deal with the problem Marshal Wade
was appointed Commander in Chief for Scotland in 1725,

32 David, Lord Ogilvy by Allan Ramsay. Lord Ogilvy was out in the '45 and was attainted. He was later pardoned on account of his youth, for he was only twenty at the time of the Rising

and under his direction six independent companies of Highlanders were formed, whose duty it was to police the area from which each company was recruited (for they had no common headquarters), and keep a vigilant eye on the movements of the Jacobites. The need for such a force is proved beyond question by the lamentable story of Lady Grange. This lady, the wife of a judge, and sister-in-law to Bobbing John, the supremely incompetent Earl of Mar who commanded the Jacobite army at Sherriffmuir, was suspected, quite wrongly, of knowing too many political secrets. In addition to this, her violent temper had for long made her odious to her husband, and on both counts he determined to be rid of her. Accordingly, one dark January night, she was forcibly removed from her lodgings in the middle of Edinburgh, and carried off to the 'vile, nasty, stinking, poor Isle of St Kilda', where she remained for no less than six years. Although it was common knowledge that Lord Lovat, along with her husband, had engineered the kidnapping, no enquiry into the extraordinary circumstances was ever made, and long before any serious attempt was made to rescue her from her odious imprisonment, the lady was dead. It is hardly to be wondered at, if, in the face of such lawlessness, the Government felt the need for stricter supervision in the north, though whether this object was wholly achieved by appointing Lord Lovat to the command of one of the newly formed companies is open to question.

From the time when they were first raised, the Independent companies wore belted plaids as their official uniform, and from the dark colouring of the tartan they became known as the Black Watch, to distinguish them from the regulars who wore red. The recruits came, in theory, from all parts of the Highlands, but in practice a large majority was drawn from Whig clans, such as Campbells, Grants and Munros. One feature that distinguished the Black Watch from all other regiments at the time was the large number of gentlemen who chose to serve as privates in the ranks. An English officer of Engineers was surprised to see that when 'these private gentlemen soldiers' were on a march, they were attended by their own ghillies, or servants, who carried their food, baggage and weapons [figures 42, 47]. The story is told how at about this time the King, having never seen a Highland soldier, expressed a desire to do so. The three handsomest privates

33 An imaginary portrait of Prince Charles Edward, artist and date unknown

in the regiment were accordingly selected, and started on their long journey south. At Aberfeldy one of the three fell ill and died; but the remaining two, John Campbell and a McGregor who went by the name of Gregor the Beautiful, continued on their journey, and eventually reached London, where they were presented to the King. To show their skill in all warlike exercises, they performed before him with broad-swords and Lochaber axes and displayed so much dexterity in the management of their weapons that as a reward, King George presented them each with a guinea. No gift could have been less welcome. They would have liked to refuse the money which as gentlemen it was beneath their dignity to accept, but as this was impossible, they took the tip and gave it instead to the porter, as they passed through the palace gates. In 1740 the Independent companies became a regiment, and, though belted plaids continued to be worn, the addition of a scarlet jacket and waistcoat brought the uniform more into line with the rest of the army.

At this stage a problem arose. What tartan was the new regiment to adopt? For to dress men who came from widely separated areas in a tartan already closely associated with one particular clan or district might well have created local jealousy. Besides, not all existing setts went well with the red of the uniform jackets. In the end an entirely new tartan was devised, which has been known ever since as the Black Watch, or Government pattern [figure 105]. It was the first tartan to be known by a specific name, or to possess a fully authenticated pedigree, and out of all the designs invented since, none has had the same far-reaching influence. From it derive the tartans of all the Highland regiments save one, and the hunting setts worn by Grants, Sutherlands, the Campbells of Argyll, and several other clans besides. But that is not all. Even today the Black Watch sett retains its astonishing popularity, and is now being put to uses that would cause its original creators to turn in their graves. They certainly never envisaged it being woven into rugs, turned into womens' trousers and carried to all parts of the world by a host of travellers who would be very much astonished to learn that the green and black checked pattern of their suitcases is of purely military origin.

When Stewart of Garth, the friend of Sir Walter Scott, came to examine the early history of the Black Watch, (of which the records had meanwhile been lost) he found

34 (*left*) James Moray of Abercairney by Jeremiah Davison, painted on the eve of the '45, showing a gentleman wearing a belted plaid. This is one of the finest pictures ever painted of that dress

35 (*right*) The Culloden tartan, so-called because a coat of this tartan was worn by a member of the Prince's suite at that battle. The sett shows the elaboration of early tartans and makes it clear that very bright colours were in every-day use at the time of the '45

36 Episode of the Rebellion, painted by David Morier immediately after the '45, was commissioned by the Government. It is of quite exceptional interest in the history of tartan, for it shows how common it was for a man to wear a jacket, plaid and hose of different tartans, none of which appear to have had any clan significance

that the Government tartan was not the only one the regiment appeared to have used. According to his information, the pipers had from the beginning worn a bright red tartan, quite unlike the sombre Government colours, to which he gave the name of 'Royal or Stewart' [figure 114]. Unfortunately, as these two words are by no means synonymous, their meaning remains obscure. It seems on the face of it highly improbable that a Hanoverian regiment, recruited from among the Whig clans, should choose deliberately to array its pipers in the red tartan of the exiled Stuarts. Besides, there is no reason to believe that such a tartan was even in existence at the time. Prince Charles Edward wore a number of different tartans while he was in Scotland, among them 'the green plaid of the Highland fashions' mentioned in the *Glasgow Courant* and a sett that is said to have resembled Drummond of Perth, but none of them could possibly be claimed as Stuart. It may be that in using the words 'Royal or Stewart' Garth wished to make a distinction between the

37 Prince Charles Edward, a drawing from a poster advertising the reward of £30,000 for his capture in 1745

tartan commonly used by all members of the clan Stewart and one that was personal to the Royal family. But if this were so, it seems strange that no one besides Garth was apparently aware of it. Among the Royal pictures at Windsor there is a portrait of George III as a boy in which a member of the House of Hanover appears in tartan for the first time [figure 20]. It shows the prince wearing the uniform of the Royal Company of Archers, and the date is 1745. If at the time there had existed a tartan more Royal than Stewart surely, for propaganda purposes alone, it would have been worn on this occasion. The problem of the pipers is further proof, if any were needed, of how frustrating a pastime the study of tartan can be. The simplest statement, the most mildly expressed opinion, is liable to stir up such a hornet's nest of contradictions that all too often one is reminded of Swift's prophecy taken down from the mouth of a man killed by the Mohocks: 'Concerning these things neither do I know, nor do ye know, but I only'. No such ambiguity can be ascribed to Stewart of Garth, but in his case the difficulty lies in deciding how much of the information was based on written evidence, and how much on hearsay. His description of military uniforms are particularly interesting because they relate to a period when Highland dress was once more in the process of evolution. The general feeling of uncertainty is reflected in many contemporary pictures, which reveal an astonishing variety of Highland fashion. In the portrait of the Macdonald children no fewer than four different tartans are displayed [figure 48], while in others there is a wide choice of trews, plaids, shawls and all tartan dresses. Even in the army a certain degree of flexibility prevailed, and the Black Watch recruits were issued with not one, but two uniforms, a belted plaid in the old style for all formal occasions, and the more modern *philabeg*. For some reason the two garments were not made of the same tartan, for while the plaids were in the Government colours, the kilts were Murray of Atholl. This sett, one of the many said to stem from the Black Watch, has a distinguished history of its own, and is remembered as the family tartan of Lord George Murray, the great Jacobite General, who was also the last man in Highland history to summon his clansmen to arms by means of the Fiery Cross.

At some point in the eighteenth century, though when exactly is far from clear, the belted plaid began to be

40 Frederick James Robertson by William Mosman. He wears a child's tartan coat

superseded by the kilt. The disadvantages of the former as a campaigning dress were already apparent at the time of the Jacobite Rising in 1715, when they attracted the notice of the Earl Marischal. After a battle, he found that many of the Highlanders could no longer remain with the army, as they had left behind them on the field of action, 'that part of their clothes which protects them most from the cold, and which likewise serves them for bed clothes' 'To explain this' he wrote, 'one must know the habit of the Highlanders, and their manner of fighting. Their clothes are composed of two short vests, the one above reaching only to their waist, the other about six inches longer; short stockings which reach not quite to their knee and no breeches; but above all they have another piece of the same stuff of about six yards long which they tie about them in such a manner that it covers their thighs, and all their body when they please, but commonly it is fixed on their left shoulder, and leaves their right arm free. This kind of mantle they throw away when they are ready to engage, to be lighter and less encumbered, and if they are beat it remains in the field.' According to other accounts, the clansmen, when they were without shields, used instead to wind their plaids round the left arm, to protect themselves against sword-thrusts and bullets.

Although it no doubt occurred to a number of people

41 Prince Charles Edward by an unknown artist. Though unlikely to have been painted from the life, it shows the Prince wearing the kind of clothes he wore in the Rising

in different districts and at different times that the design of the plaid could be improved upon, in only one case has the name of the reformer been preserved, and he, curiously enough, was an Englishman. Some time after the '15, an iron foundry was established in Glengarry, of which a man called Rawlinson was appointed the manager. He, in turn, had a friend, a tailor by profession, who used often to visit him and who took a great interest in the native dress of the country. One day, while the two of them were sitting together by the fire, a Highlander entered the room, wearing a belted plaid soaked by the rain which, to the tailor's surprise, he did not offer to take off. Being a curious man, he enquired the reason,

and found that what he had assumed to be a kind of cloak, was in fact a complete outfit made of a single piece of material, and pleated round the waist by hand every time it was put on. It seemed to him then, that if the plaid were divided into two, the pleats of the lower half could be sewn, and so kept permanently in position. This would allow the upper half to be put on and taken off at will. The idea made an instant appeal to Rawlinson, who was himself in the habit of wearing Highland dress, and within two days he appeared wearing for the first time, the 'little kilt'. When McDonell of Glengarry saw the advantages of the new design, he too adopted it for his own, and through him the fashion spread

43 The third Duke of Perth by Allan Ramsay, one of the Jacobite commanders in the '45, who was mortally wounded at Culloden and died on board ship on the way to France

44 About the turn of the nineteenth century Scotland was becoming fashionable; Cœuriot wore this costume for his role of MacGregor in the opera *La Dame du Lac*

45 Norman, twenty-second Chief of Macleod, by Allan Ramsay. This portrait shows a Highland chief wearing trews and a plaid, a costume often worn by chiefs because it was a more satisfactory riding-dress than a kilt

46 A popular idea of Highland costume; Madame Montano, the opera singer, wore this dress for her part of Malcolm in *La Dame du Lac*

rapidly to other parts of the district. The truth of this story has often been disputed, and to this day there are many ardent nationalists who cannot bring themselves to admit that an Englishman should have had a hand in the development of what has now become almost a national institution. Such feelings are understandable, but they are based on a misconception. It is not suggested that Rawlinson was the sole, or even the earliest, begetter of the kilt, but only that in his case, the facts are fully known. Donald Macleod, one-time sergeant in the Royal Scots, whose autobiography was·published in 1791, had a memory that went back nearly a hundred years to the great Highland famine of 1698, and he remembered vividly the

47 (*below centre*) Belted plaids worn as cloaks against the rain

clothes he wore as a boy: 'a woolen shirt, a kilt or short petticoat, and a short coat or rather waist-coat, reaching down and buttoning at the wrist'. This was in Inverness, but in Breadalbane, on the other hand, the belted plaid was still in use at the end of the eighteenth century, and possibly even later. All that can be said with any certainty is that the fashion that came with such dramatic suddenness to Glengarry was spreading to other parts of the Highlands at about the same time, but in some districts more rapidly than in others.

Although no less an authority than Sir Walter Scott gave it as his opinion that after the Union tartan was adopted as the national emblem, it is not at all clear to

48 The Macdonald children by Jeremiah Davison. This is a particularly interesting picture because none of the four tartans in it resemble any modern Macdonald sett

what extent this was true before the '45. Among Jacobites of both sexes it was certainly widely worn, even in the south of Scotland, where tartan shawls were for long a fashionable item of female attire, but taking Scotland as a whole, the popular craze for tartan did not begin until a much later date. It was only after the '45 grew from an awkward political incident into a national legend that tartans began to have a universal appeal.

So much has been written about the last Jacobite Rising, and so many contradictory opinions expressed, that it is

49 The Pinch of Snuff, painted by William Delacour in 1750, one of the most important early pictures of military uniforms. The officer wears a belted plaid of an unusual coloured tartan, while the rest of his uniform is of the 1742 *Cloathing Book* pattern, now preserved in the War Office, London

easy to forget how modest were its origins, and what a small part of the nation was involved in the affair at all. When Murray of Broughton went to Paris in 1744, and had his momentous interview with the Prince, 'at the great stables in the Tuileries', Charles told him that 'in all events he was determined to come the following summer to Scotland, though with a single foot man'. He then proceeded to enquire what support he might expect to receive in Scotland, and Murray's reply was that 'the Duke of Perth [figure 43], Lochiel, Keppoch, Clanranald, the

A Highland Piper. A Highlander in his Regimentals. A Highland Drummer.

The beautiful Dress used by the Highlanders is in great part the Ancient Roman Habit: For Tacitus tells us that the celebrated Roman Consul Agricola to soften this fierce and warlike People by his good Address prevailed upon them, not only to learn the Roman Language, but to accept the Habit, and build Houses and Publick Buildings of all sorts.

50 After the passing of the Dress Act in 1747, the only place where tartan could be worn was in the army. The pipes were similarly banned. The author of this print subscribed to the view that Highland dress 'is in great part the Ancient Roman Habit'

Stewarts, MacDonalds of Glengarry with Cluny and Struan. Robertson's people were all he could rely upon with any certainty from the West Highlands'; in all, four thousand men at the most. Another estimate put the total number of clansmen capable of bearing arms at 20,550, of whom a little over half were known to be Jacobites. The names of twenty-nine known clans were listed. When one remembers that today there are in the region of six hundred clan or family tartans, it will be seen that the clan system has undergone considerable development in the course of the past two hundred years. Notwithstanding the lack of encouragement he received, the Prince sailed for Scotland, and landed at Eriskay. On August 19 the Royal standard was raised at Glenfinnan, where a memorial now marks the spot. It was in the disguise of a minister that Charles Edward returned to his lost

51 Sir Stuart Threipland Bt of Fingask by William Delacour, *c.* 1755. This is a very good picture of the old *philabeg*, showing how full it was sometimes worn

inheritance, to be met by the doubts and forebodings of the chiefs. Macdonald of Boisdale advised him to go home, only to receive the answer, 'I am come home'. In a letter to his father he announced his intention of gaining immortal honour or perishing, as he put it, 'sord in hand'. The Prince's spelling was always erratic but he was not lacking in spirit. Throughout the campaign that followed, the Jacobites fought under the command of their chiefs in clan regiments, and from the many eyewitness accounts, both friendly and hostile, that have come down to us, it is possible to form an accurate picture both of their dress and manners. The Prince, contrary to popular belief, was never seen in a kilt before Culloden, though he wore one during his later wanderings [figures 33, 37]. When he rode into Edinburgh he was attired in red velvet breeches, a green velvet bonnet with a white cockade, and boots.

52 Robert Grant of Lurg, who served in the Independent companies. Anon, *c.* 1760

At the Scottish United Services Museum in Edinburgh is preserved an actual suit said to have belonged to him. It consists of a tartan jacket in seven colours, with collar and cuffs of purple velvet, and red and green diced trews. Although most of the Jacobite officers favoured trews, at Blair Castle there is an interesting picture of Lord George Murray wearing a red belted plaid, striped in black, with a targe, or Highland shield, on one arm. The occupation of Edinburgh by the Prince's forces not unnaturally led to an immediate fashion in all things Highland, and one enterprizing firm of merchants hastened to satisfy the demand by advertising its stock of tartan 'of the newest patterns'.

It is hardly necessary to add that this example has been widely copied since. The Edinburgh tailors were probably right in thinking that the quality of some Highland wardrobes left much to be desired. In 1715 the Minister of Mulmearn had watched part of the army, 'those who joined the Pretender, from the most remote parts of the Highlands, march past his house, wearing only long coats of one colour, without shirts, shoes, stockings or breeches. Thirty years later the clansmen were less scantily clad, but the appearance they presented was no less startling.

53 The Hon William Gordon, painted in 1766 by Pompeo Batoni, wearing the Huntly district tartan, still worn today

54 Macbeth and Banquo, painted by Woolett after Zuccarelli

After Culloden a Swiss artist called David Morier, who had previously been employed making accurate recordings of regimental uniforms throughout the army, was commissioned by the Government to paint a picture showing Highlanders in action. The result was *Episode of the Rebellion*, in which a group of clansmen is shown attacking the lines of Barrell's Blues (now the 4th King's Own) at Culloden [figure 36]. It is said that in order to assist his researches a number of Highland prisoners were put at his disposal, and these he painted as he found them, some in belted plaids, and others in trews or *philabegs*. As a commentary on Highland dress in general, and tartan in particular, Morier's picture is of quite exceptional interest. It shows, among other things, how common it was at the time for a man to wear a jacket, plaid and hose of entirely different tartans, none of which appear to have had any clan significance. It is also worth remembering that in the early days of tartan designs a very wide range of colours was used, and that the distinction now drawn between the red 'dress' tartans, and the more muted greens and browns of the 'hunting' setts is as modern as it is artificial. Among the pre-1745 tartans red appears to have been as popular a colour as green, and was worn as much for hunting and in war as it was on more formal occasions. The surviving fragment of the Culloden coat, so-called because it was found on the body of an unknown Highlander killed at that battle, shows both the high degree of sophistication that the weaver's art could achieve, and how small a part the notion of camouflage played in the dress of the clans [figure 35]. Whether clan tartans were in existence at the time of the '45 is a point that will always be disputed, and on which even the Morier picture offers no certain guidance. It is true that all his Highlanders are shown wearing different tartans, but this might be due to the circumstance that the prisoners who served him as models were drawn from different clans. Even the fact that individual Highlanders wore a combination of several different tartans is not in itself conclusive, as it is quite possible that, in the course of the campaign, the clothes belonging to the dead were appropriated by the survivors. What is much more significant is that none of the tartans known to have been worn by the Jacobite chiefs of the time can be identified with any clan tartans in use today. Even the waistcoat that Macdonald of Kingsburgh gave to Charles Edward is

45

55 Scottish rural life seen through English eyes; a caricature of Scottish drovers

56 Hugh, twelfth Earl of Eglinton, in the uniform of the 42nd Regiment (Black Watch), after Copley

quite unlike any modern Macdonald sett.

A passage from the Lockhart papers shows the difficulty experienced by the Highlanders themselves in telling friends from foe. In 1745 a party of Macdonalds, fighting on the Jacobite side, found themselves face to face with the men commanded by Sir Alexander Macdonald, who supported King George, and as both sides wore the same clan badge, a sprig of heather in their bonnets, the only difference lay in the colour of their cockades. Nothing is said about dress, but had the tartan worn by the various branches of the clan Macdonald presented the same striking differences then as it does now, it is inconceivable that Lockhart should not have mentioned it.

Tartan in the Army

57 A mounted officer in a Highland Regiment, 1743

BY 1746 THE RISING WAS OVER, and the Prince who had landed in Scotland with such high hopes only a year before became a hunted fugitive, skulking in caves and on the open hillside, a price of thirty thousand pounds on his head. The reward went unclaimed, and after a series of harrowing adventures, he finally sailed for France, in 'a short coat of coarse, black frieze, tartan trews, and

47

over them a belted plaid'. It was, as Lord Seafield had remarked of the Union half a century before, the end of an old song.

Twice in thirty years the Government had been called upon to quell a Highland uprising, and after the second attempt it was resolved to make an example of those who for so long had defied the royal authority. In 1746 an Act was passed making it illegal for Highlanders either to own or carry arms. It was not the first time that such legislation had been attempted, for already on two previous occasions, in 1718 and again in 1726, the Government had tried to enforce the surrender of all weapons. In both cases the clansmen had shown themselves most willing to comply with the demand, but as the only weapons they chose to give up were those too old or broken to be of any further use, it was not felt that either of these experiments had been wholly successful. The new Act put an end to all further evasion. This was bad enough, but worse was to follow. A year later the Dress Act was passed, making it illegal for any man or boy 'to wear or put on the clothes commonly called Highland clothes, that is to say, the plaid, *philabeg* or little kilt, trowse, shoulder belt or any part whatsoever of what peculiarly belongs to the Highland garb; and that no tartan or party-coloured plaid or stuff shall be used for great-coats or for upper-coats'. The punishment for a first offence was six months' imprisonment, and for a second, transportation 'to any of His Majesty's plantations beyond the seas—there to remain for the space of seven years'. Even the pipes were banned, the Duke of Cumberland having formed the opinion on first hand evidence that they were 'an instrumente of war'.

For thirty-five years the hated Act remained on the Statute Book, and during that time the only place where tartan might legally be worn was in the army. Even those clans who had fought on the Government side were subject to the new rules, and so strictly were they at first enforced that one young man from Ardchattan, who had been convicted of wearing one of the prohibited garments, was, without more ado, drafted into the army for service in America. Another, who had never even heard of the Act, found himself convicted of the same crime, and was thrown protesting into Inverness jail. Trousers were so unpopular among the clansmen, that for long journeys, rather than put them on they preferred to hang them over

58 John Macdonald, piper to Glenaladale

59 This conversation-piece shows John, fourth Duke of Atholl, and his family, painted in 1780 by David Allan

their shoulders, and wear instead a makeshift skirt (made of anything but tartan) or the forbidden *philabeg*, stitched down the middle. In place of swords they took to carrying sticks, and as a substitute for the dirk, a shorter knife called a *skean dhu* was adopted, small enough to be easily concealed in a pocket or stuck in the top of a stocking [figure 96]. Meanwhile, in the absence of other employment, a number of Highlanders enlisted in the army, and so

SCOTTISH SOLDIERS *of the* HIGHLANDS.   *An* HIGHLAND OF

60 Scottish soldiers in 1793

ER _and_ SERJEANT.

successful did the experiment prove, that in the space of six years, no less than nine line regiments and six of Fencibles were raised. Some of these were sent to Flanders, where the unfamiliar uniforms excited a good deal of comment, and were made the subject of numerous illustrations [figures 42, 47]. An unknown correspondent in the _Vienna Gazette_ described the Highlanders as 'running wild, like savages but capable of becoming good and faithful subjects when converted from heathenism. They are caught in the mountains when young; the men are of low stature and most of them old or very young, and the officers are all young and handsome'. Seeing how great a demand there was for Highland recruits, some of the clan chiefs, who since the time of the '45 had been languishing in exile, felt that the moment had come to strike a bargain with the Government by offering to raise troops from among their former clansmen. Many were able to secure a pardon for themselves, and in some cases even to buy back their forfeited estates. Thus, Fraser's Highlanders were commanded by the Hon. Simon Fraser, whose father, Lord Lovat, had been executed for his part in the Rising, and of the sixteen hundred men he recruited, nearly half came from the Lovat estates. These early regiments wore a number of different tartans in a variety of colours, whose origin are now hard to trace, but gradually as some units were disbanded and others formed, the anomalies disappeared and the Black Watch or Government sett was accepted as the standard military pattern. Although, at first sight there might not appear to be any obvious resemblance between the tartans worn respectively by the Gordon Highlanders, the Seaforth, and the Black Watch, the only difference is in the colour of the overstripes. These are red and white in the case of the Seaforth and yellow for the Gordon Highlanders [figure 105]. A letter written in 1793 by William Forsyth, a manufacturer from Aberdeen, throws an interesting light on the origin of the last-named tartan. 'When I had the honour of communicating with His Grace The Duke of Gordon, he was desirous to have patterns of the 42nd Regiment plaid, with a small yellow stripe properly placed. Enclosed 3 patterns of the 42nd plaid all having yellow stripes. From this I hope His Grace will fix on some of the three stripes—when the plaids are worn the yellow stripes will be square and regular. I imagine the yellow stripes will appear very lively.'

61 A portrait of Sir Evan MacGregor, painted by Raeburn in 1797, a very pretty picture of a child in a tartan suit

62 A Highland shepherd and his dog, from W. Pyne's *The Costume of Great Britain*

Out of all the Highland regiments, only one can claim to possess a tartan that is not in any way connected with the Black Watch. When the 79th (Cameron Highlanders) were first raised, their Colonel, Alan Cameron of Erracht, was reluctant to put his men into the Government sett and consequently a new one was devised for them by his

63 The famous fiddler Neil Gow, painted by Raeburn. The tartan called Gow derives from him

64 The *Cloathing Book*, drawn up by the War Office in 1742, recorded the exact details of all British Army uniforms; a private in the Black Watch in his belted plaid

mother [figure 105]. The fact that her design was based on one already in existence at the time and widely known by the name of Macdonald, is an indication of the way in which clan tartans had developed since the middle of the eighteenth century.

In the early days of the regiment, a firm of manufacturers

CREED'S
Theatrical Combats,
in the
LADY of the LAKE
N.º 23

FITZ.JAMES. *M.ʳ Huntley.*   RODERIC

Publ.ᵈ July 1819, by G. Creed, Exeter Street, Strand.

54

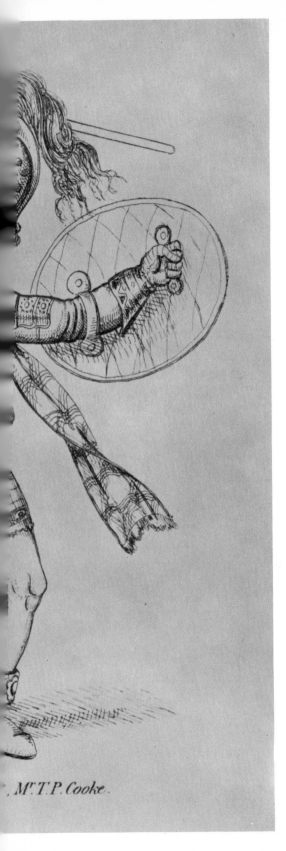

from Paisley supplied the 79th with its tartan which was then a somewhat comfortless material, very harsh to the touch, the yarns being made from 'combed' wool. By the middle of the nineteenth century the officers had abandoned the hard weave in favour of a softer material, a tartan made from 'carded' wool, but the rank and file in all the Highland regiments continued to wear the old hard tartan for a further thirty years, until the intervention of Queen Victoria led to its abolition. 'In the autumn of 1872, Her Majesty having noticed that a detachment of the 93rd (the Guard of Honour at Ballater) wore kilts and plaids of hard tartan, and that after a march in wind and rain the men's knees were much scratched and cut by the sharp edge of the tartan, the Queen was graciously pleased to direct that soft instead of hard tartan be in future supplied to Highland regiments.'

The tradition that all Scottish regiments should wear tartan has by now taken such a firm hold on the popular imagination that one is sometimes in danger of forgetting the many transformations that military uniform has undergone since first a regular army was established in this country. When the Highland regiments were first recruited, it is true that the kilt was worn by all ranks, and indeed the fact that it was then illegal for any civilian to be seen in Highland dress was one reason why so many Highlanders of all classes were willing, as the phrase went, 'to take the King's shilling'. In the beginning, as has already been shown, the regiments were run on traditional lines, and as recruitment was on a geographical basis, they differed very little from the clan levies of an earlier age. The 73rd, whose colonel was a Mackenzie, had nineteen officers of the same name serving in the regiment, and in the 98th, of which the Duke of Argyll was colonel, seventeen Campbells held commissions.

Although Highland uniform was officially sanctioned by the army, it was not accepted without a struggle. When Fraser's Highlanders went to Canada in the 1770's, strong pressure was brought to bear on them to adopt the ordinary dress of a Line regiment. This was resisted and throughout the campaign they clung to the traditional tartan, but the Black Watch, who were serving with them at the time, found that for work in 'Battoes' (boats) the

65 Sir Walter Scott's *Waverley* novels contributed to the Celtic revival; a play and an opera were based on his poem the *Lady of the Lake*, written in 1810

66 A modern dirk, mounted in silver with cairngorms

67 Neil McLean, piper to the Highland Society *c.* 1800, a stipple engraving by William Craig. His dirk is very similar to the modern one

68 A modern dirk for dress occasions

69 Doctor Nathaniel Spens, painted by Sir Henry Raeburn in 1791 in the uniform of the Royal Company of Archers

70 Prints were made of the leading actors in *Rob Roy*; Helen MacGregor haranguing the army

71 A line engraving of Farquhar Shaw, one of the Black Watch mutineers shot in the Tower in 1743

kilt was not without its disadvantages, and as a temporary expedient they took to wearing breeches made out of old tents. The outbreak of the Napoleonic Wars forced the army to expand, and as new recruits came in and the casualties mounted, the Highland regiments began to lose something of their original character. To the Lowland Scots and Englishmen who now joined the ranks, Highland dress was nothing more than a bizarre anachronism and quite alien to their own traditions. It was also an opinion strongly held in military circles that the kilt was not only an indecent garment, but a most unsuitable one to wear in a hot climate. As there was no easy way of resolving these difficulties, some regiments gave up wearing tartan altogether. In 1809, five of them adopted the trousers and shakos of a Line regiment. Out of the remaining seven, five retained their kilts, while two went into tartan trews. During the Peninsular campaigns it became the practice for officers in kilted regiments to dress in blue or grey pantaloons. In the Cameron Highlanders their uniform consisted of grey trousers and black gaiters. It was not until a much later date that the kilt was worn for anything except Reviews and Guards of Honour, though there is a story of two kilted officers from the regiment attending the great ball given by the Duchess of Richmond in Brussels on the eve of Waterloo. It is said they were obliged to leave so hurriedly that when they marched south to Quatre Bras, they were still in their dancing shoes.

The Camerons were not the only regiment whose officers commonly wore trousers or tartan trews in preference to the kilt. In Wellington's army they were encouraged, in the interests of efficiency, to ride as much as possible, and this may well have given rise to a fashion that soon spread throughout the kilted regiments, the 78th (Seaforths) alone resisting the pressure. Although some Highland regiments wore brown Holland tunics, the earliest form of khaki, during the Indian Mutiny, the colour found no favour with the purists, and it was only at the end of the nineteenth century that the traditional red was finally abandoned. Even so, the writing was on the wall, and the experiences of the army in the Crimea only served to underline the fact that the lovely and romantic uniforms of a peacetime army were ill-adapted to serve the needs of nineteenth-century war. In the course of that ill-managed campaign, the commissariat broke down

72 The costume worn by Rob Roy in the play that was based on Sir Walter Scott's novel of that name

utterly, all attempt at uniformity of dress had perforce to be given up, and some of the outfits that Her Majesty's soldiers wore were of an eccentricity that has rarely been equalled since. One photograph shows a group of Black Watch officers, in which the most noticeable figure is wearing an ill-fitting tartan jacket over a white waistcoat, an outsize bow tie and trews.

By the middle of Queen Victoria's reign, all the regiments who had given up Highland dress in 1809 were wearing it again, though the tartans they assumed on the second occasion were not necessarily the same as those originally chosen. The 91st (Argyll and Sutherland Highlanders) were confronted with an unexpected difficulty, for only after the Queen offered to restore their kilts, was it discovered that no-one knew which tartan to wear. In the original letters it was referred to merely as 'the green tartan with the blue line', approved for the regiment in 1794.

The end of the century saw the beginning of the South African war, where for the first time the Highland regiments wore a kind of khaki apron, as camouflage, over the front of their kilts. In 1914 this was extended to cover the whole of the tartan. Although tartan was worn intermittently during the 1939-45 war, to-day neither trews nor the kilt is any longer worn on active service, and in times of war there is now nothing to distinguish the Scottish regiments from other units in the army except the bonnets that they alone are still entitled to wear, and the small tartan patches on the sleeves of their battle dress blouses.

The association of Lowland regiments with tartan is not an old one, but it is nevertheless interesting, and deserves to be considered. In the seventeenth and eighteenth centuries when they were first raised, it was not envisaged by anyone that Lowland regiments should be dressed in tartan. After 1881, however, all Lowland regiments, with the exception of the Scots Guards, went into what are now called trews, a name in itself misleading, for the straight tartan trousers in use to-day bear almost no resemblance to the trews of the eighteenth century. The latter consisted of a closely-fitting pair of breeches and stockings cut all in one piece, and worn usually with garters. At first, the different regiments all took the same tartan, the ubiquitous Government sett, but latterly a reaction has set in against such uninspired uniformity, and at the present time almost all of them wear the setts now associated with the names of their founders. One cannot but reflect how astonished these would be to see their men so strangely habited.

In all Scottish battalions there are pipers who do not necessarily wear the regimental tartan but the Royal Stewart instead. Although the pipes have always had a mixed reception outside Scotland, one critic going so far as to describe them as 'a useless relic of the barbarous ages, and not in any manner calculated to discipline troops', it must be allowed that their popularity has not been entirely confined to the Scottish regiments. Before 1947 no less than forty Indian Army pipe-bands were in existence, and for a short time one of these, astonishing as it may seem, was mounted. The pipers rode on grey horses, with the reins attached to their stirrups. Many of the bands

73 James Macdonald, Younger of Dalness, painted by Captain Mackenzie. From a line engraving by W. Pouny, c. 1820

74 An officer in the Battalion Company,
Black Watch *c.* 1790

were equipped with tartan-covered Scottish pipes, and in
some regiments the pipers also wore plaids in different
clan setts. Occasionally something more original was
preferred. The blue and yellow tartan known as Johore
is one example of a design made exclusively for an Indian
frontier regiment [figure 105]. In many other parts of the
Commonwealth and in South Africa, there are regiments
with Scottish names, whose uniform still consists of trews
or the kilt.

The Celtic Revival

75 A Child of the Mist, from the fashionable drama, *Montrose* or *The Children of the Mist*, 1822

IT HAS BEEN SHOWN how the Dress Act confined the use of tartan for over thirty years to the army. By the time it was repealed in 1783, the structure of Highland society had altered so much that in the interval many of the old customs and traditions had disappeared for ever. Already the drift of population overseas, that was later to grow into the open scandal of the Clearances, had begun, and everywhere there was a growing feeling of uncertainty, if not of despair [figure 105]. It was the avowed purpose of the Act to break the link uniting the people of the Highlands to their traditional form of dress, and in this it succeeded only too well. Something was destroyed in the years of Proscription that could not afterwards be re-created. In spite of the many devoted efforts made during the nineteenth century to revive and popularize Highland dress, it became less and less the everyday

76 John, second Marquis of Bute, by Sir Henry Raeburn. The sitter wears the clothes of a Regency dandy, with a Highland cloak instead of a greatcoat

wear of fishermen and crofters, and more and more a conscious manifestation of national pride. The description given by the Rev. Alexander Sage of his childhood days in the Manse of Kildonan at the turn of the century reads like an echo of a more peaceful age, when set against the grim reality of the Clearances (three thousand from Invernesshire, ten thousand from the West and the Isles, fifteen thousand in Sutherland). 'Both my sisters' he recalled 'were dressed in tartan gowns of home manufacture. Their hair was braided on the forehead, and saturated with pomatum, and they were made to look, upon the whole, like two young damsels from a Highland nursery, making their first appearance in public life. My brother and I were clothed in the same identical tartan, but of a make and habit suitable to our age and sex. This was a kilt after the most approved fashion, surmounted with a jacket fitted tight to the body and to which the kilt was affixed by a tailor's seam. The jacket and kilt, open in front, were shut in upon our persons with yellow buttons... we were furnished with white worsted stockings, tied below the knee with red garters, of which Malvolio himself would have approved. Our feet were inserted into Highland brogues, while our heads were combed and powdered with flour, as a substitute for the hair powder which was the distinguishing mark of all the swells of that fashionable age.'

It is one of the many paradoxes of Scottish history that the age which witnessed the gradual decay of the Highlands at the same time created an interest in the subject that even now is not yet dead. Why should this have been so? No easy explanation is possible, but there are indications that ought not to be ignored. When *Waverley* was first published, it bore as its subtitle the words 'or Tis Sixty Years Since' and it is beyond question that one factor in the book's phenomenal success was Scott's admirable sense of timing. Had the world of Fergus Mac Ivor and the Gifted Gilfillan been no more than a masterly reconstruction of ancient history, it could not have evoked the response that it did. And had it been written even fifty years later, it would no longer have been possible to span the gulf that divided the old, turbulent Scotland of the eighteenth century from the age of John Stuart Mill and Sir James Simpson. It was Scott's happy fortune to be born at a time when the sorrows of the '45 had not yet passed into legend, but were still a living memory. As a

63

77 (*above*) William, eleventh Duke of Hamilton, painted by Richard Buckner, The Duke is portrayed in the Byronic manner, in an open-necked shirt

78 (*right*) Sir John Sinclair of Ulbster, by Sir Henry Raeburn, in the uniform of the Rothesay and Caithness Fencibles, of which he was Colonel Commandant. A great authority on Highland dress, Sir John maintained that the most ancient form of it was trews, not the kilt, and his regiment was dressed accordingly

child he was introduced to one who had witnessed the execution of the Jacobite prisoners at Carlisle and all his life he remembered how his father had flung from the window of their Edinburgh house the tea cup out of which Murray of Broughton, Prince Charles' renegade secretary, had so much as dared to drink. It would, of course, be foolish to pretend that Sir Walter was alone responsible for the

79 (*above*) Leading characters in *Montrose*, whose costumes reflected the current interest in all things Scottish

80 (*right*) George IV, in a kilt of red tartan, by Sir David Wilkie. George IV is known to have worn Royal Stewart tartan at a *lévée* at Holyrood-house in 1820, the first time a crowned head wore this tartan. Wilkie may have had this in mind

Celtic revival, but it was he who gave it impetus and lent it distinction. When in 1822 King George IV decided to visit his northern kingdom, a journey no crowned king since Charles I had made, it set the seal on his achievement.

In spite of an element of burlesque that was never wholly absent from the proceedings, the occasion passed

65

81 Highland Regiments marching in Edinburgh in 1822, an engraving after J. M. W. Turner

off astonishingly well. The King set sail from Greenwich in the *Royal George*, towed by the *Comet* steam packet. At Scarborough the Mayor and Corporation hoped to present a loyal address and were waiting in a boat for the purpose, but the *Comet* was going too fast to stop, and instead they were obliged to tender their greetings on the end of a long stick. Like so many other visitors, before and since, the King reached Leith in a downpour, which prevented him from proceeding at once to Edinburgh. The next day he drove in state to Holyrood. Scott also took part in the procession, dressed in Campbell trews, with his coachman in a blonde wig. It says much for the stamina of this stout gentleman of sixty that for over a week he did his best to play the part of that other prince who, less than a century before, had set the whole town ablaze. Every day there were drawing-rooms, processions, banquets, and the Highlands came into their own again when chiefs like Glengarry paraded the streets and the King himself was heard to propose the toast of 'Health to the Chieftains and Clans'. But the grand climacteric of the visit was the *lévée* held at Holyrood, when to the gratification of all, His Majesty appeared in a kilt of the Royal Stewart tartan [figure 80]. It was unfortunate that at the same function a portly London alderman called Sir William Curtis, who had hitherto worn nothing more controversial than white trousers and a frock-coat, entirely lost his head and spurred on, perhaps, by the presence of so many Highland chiefs, assumed an outfit that, as a parody of the King's, could hardly have been bettered. Even the tartan was the same. 'A portentous apparition' is how Scott described the astonishing spectacle. For him the visit was not one of unalloyed pleasure, as the whole weight of organizing what was in effect a national pageant fell on his shoulders, and it was only when it was over that he could look upon it as a success. His minor worries included a meeting with the poet Crabbe, whom he found addressing a group of puzzled chieftains in fluent French, under the impression that they were foreigners. On leaving Scotland the King gave a promise that the forfeited Jacobite peerages would be restored but the graceful gesture, that cost so little and yet counted for something, did nothing to propitiate Byron who viewed the expedition as nothing more than a ridiculous charade:

Teach them the decencies of good threescore;
Cure them of tours, hussars and Highland dresses;
Tell them that youth once gone returns no more,
That hired huzzars redeem no land's distresses;
Tell them Sir William Curtis is a bore,
Too dull even for the dullest of excesses—
The witless Falstaff of a hoary Hall,
A fool whose bells have ceased to ring at all.

It is not too much to say that George IV's visit to Edinburgh represents a turning point in the history of Highland dress. Before him, no king had even worn a tartan categorically claimed to be Royal Stewart, and in the absence of any positive proof, it may be seriously doubted whether such a tartan had long been in existence.

There is another important point to consider. With the coming of the Industrial Revolution it became possible for the first time to produce with perfect accuracy large quantities of material woven to the same design, and this development without a doubt played a major part in the standardization of clan setts. Unfortunately, at the very time when district and clan tartans were beginning to emerge from the mythological past and acquire a reputable

82 A romantic portrait of John Wilkie of Foulden, in the uniform of the Royal Company of Archers, painted by Denis Dighton c. 1822

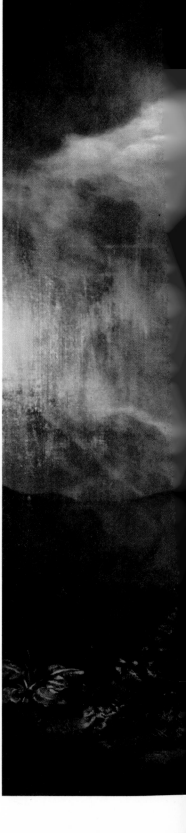

83 Colonel Alasdair Macdonnell of Glengarry, by Sir Henry Raeburn. He killed Flora Macdonald's grandson in a duel, and was a friend of Sir Walter Scott

pedigree of their own, the Highlands were caught up in the tempest of the '45. For a generation thereafter no tartan was openly made or worn, and it cannot be doubted that during that time, a number of known setts either disappeared or were altered beyond recognition. Until the publication of *The Scottish Gäel* in 1831 no one had attempted a description of the tartans already in existence. The author of this remarkable work was James Logan, and in order to assist his researches, he spent several years wandering round Scotland, visiting the places where tartan was made. Stirling, he found, was a great centre of the industry, the town being especially celebrated for a very fine scarlet weave known as Stirling tartan. At the nearby village of Bannockburn lived an old man known as 'the Lord Lyon of Tartan heraldry' from the great knowledge he had of the various patterns. *The Scottish Gäel* records the existence of fifty-five different setts, all of which are accurately described. Logan never claimed that the list was exhaustive, and when that controversial work, the *Vestiarium Scoticum*, came out a few years later, it contained illustrations of seventy-five tartans. Whether the majority of these were invented for the occasion or did in fact possess the pedigree that was claimed for them is a question still hotly disputed, but one thing that is not in doubt is that, at the time, a great many tartans were being invented, many of which are now looked upon almost in the light of family heirlooms. In a letter to Sir Walter Scott, Sir Thomas Dick Lauder gives a lively account of the mood prevailing in 1829. 'In these times of rage for tartans when the most uncouth coats of many colours are every day invented, manufactured, christened after particular names and worn as genuine, a book of this kind (the *Vestiarium Scoticum*) containing authority so valuable must become extremely popular. At present a woeful want of knowledge in the subject prevails. Some of the clans are at this moment ignorantly disputing for the right to the same tartans which in fact belong to none of them, but are merely modern inventions for clothing Regimental Highlanders. Hardly does one of the clans now wear its tartan with its legitimate setts, stripes and spranges perfect in all their parts.'

Since Sir Thomas wrote in praise of the *Vestiarium Scoticum* the attentions it has received have been of a less flattering kind. Its authors were two brothers who called themselves the Sobieski Stuarts, and claimed to be

84 The macnab by Sir Henry Raeburn

85 Both the sitter and artist of this charming portrait are unknown; it was painted c. 1830. It shows a child's complete tartan coat

the legitimate heirs of the royal house of Stuart [figure 90]. When it was objected that this could hardly be so, as Prince Charles Edward, though married, had left no legitimate children, their answer was that, on the contrary, one son had been born to him, who for fear of Hanoverian plots had been handed over to an English admiral called Allen at a very early age, and brought up as his own son. It is certainly true that this child, whose name was Thomas Allen, was their father. Very little is known of the brothers' early life, but according to their own account they were educated abroad, and served at one time in Napoleon's army, where Charles, the younger of the two, was decorated for bravery in the field. They subsequently came to London, learnt Gaelic, and then made their way to Scotland, where they were received with deference, first by Lord Moray [figure 88], and later by Lord Lovat, who invited them to settle on any part of his estates that they might fancy. They chose for their abode a small island in the Beauly river, and there a new house was built for them, and they gave themselves up to painting, scholarship and sport. Impostors though they

86 The Cock of the North, portrait of George, fifth Duke of Gordon, by George Sanders

must have been, they did know a great deal about the Highlands, and through their extensive knowledge of Gaelic were able to acquire much of the information contained in their published works. In 1842, the first of these, the *Vestiarium*, appeared. It was a treatise on tartan, supposedly based on three ancient manuscripts, of which the brothers claimed to be the possessors. It need hardly be added that no outsider was ever permitted to see them. The book was very handsomely produced and sold at ten guineas. Even at that price its popularity was such that one astute Inverness citizen was said to have paid for his copy by hiring it out to the many who wished to see it. It is still far from clear why the brothers, who were scholars and capable of better things, should have lent themselves to an idiotic fraud. Possibly their faith in the manuscripts sprang from the same mad, mysterious source as their belief in their own kingly descent. The *Vestiarium* was assailed, and rightly assailed, on all sides. Its origins were dubious. Its theories were absurd. All of which may well be true, but it must also be remembered that with all its faults, the book remains the sole authority

87 Alexander Cumming Dewar of Vogrie, a watercolour by Boggit, 1833

88 John, twelfth Earl of Moray, was the first host of the Sobieski Stuarts in Scotland. He entertained them at Darnaway. Portrait by Sir John Watson Gordon

71

89 The Marchioness of Queensbury, painted by Sir William Beechey, wears a tartan hat, reflecting the popularity of tartan in the early nineteenth century

for a number of well-known tartans, and very pretty ones, still in use today. The brothers' next work was *The Costume of the Clans*, a monumental study of Highland dress, and in contrast to their first work, 'a perfect marvel of industry and ability'.

For several years the strange pair, one of whom was now married, continued to live on their land-locked island. During that time they wrote two further books, *Lays of the Deer Forest*, and a romantic autobiography entitled

90 John and Charles Sobieski Stuart claimed to be the legitimate grandson of Prince Charles Edward. This self-portrait was painted at Eileen Aigas, the house given to them by Lord Lovat when they settled on his estates

Tales of the Century, in which veiled allusions to their own Royal past, a deep affection for Highland life and much forgotten folklore were inextricably interwoven. Finally, the house of Eilean Aigas was given up, they moved to Austria, then back to England, and one of the last glimpses that history affords of them is of two old gentlemen, handsome and courteous as ever, sitting side by side in the reading room of the British Museum with knives, pens and paper weights spread out in front of them,

73

91 The elaborate Highland clothes of George and Hugh Brodie illustrate the Romantic revival of the nineteenth century. Portrait by James Currie, 1846

all embellished by a small gold crown. It is easy to laugh at the Sobieski Stuarts, but whichever way one looks at it their achievement was remarkable. In spite of the fact that roads were very bad, reliable witnesses lacking and that much of their information came to them through the medium of a foreign language, they nevertheless suceeded in collecting a vast amount of material on the dress, customs and history of the Highlands, at a time when all three were in danger of being forgotten. In the course of their travels they stayed often at Inverie, the house belonging to Alasdair Macdonnell of Glengarry, and from him, or his family, they had confirmation of the story already referred to in these chapters, concerning Mr Rawlinson, one-time manager of the Invergarry iron-works, and his kilt. Glengarry was a great figure in his day, the friend of Sir Walter Scott to whom he gave the deerhound Maida, and it is to him that Scott probably went for

92 Family Picnic on the Culbin Sands, signed 'W. B. 1846', showing that tartan was beginning to be used not only for clothes but for rugs. Anyone who has ever picnicked in Scotland will recognise the weather

inspiration when he drew the character of Fergus Mac Ivor in *Waverley* [figure 83]. He was a man of very ferocious temper, and had once fought a duel, on slight provocation, with a grandson of Flora Macdonald, in which the young man was killed. Public opinion was aroused, and it was only with difficulty that he escaped the legal conse- quences of his crime. Glengarry was the last Highland chief to maintain the state of an earlier and more savage age. He wore Highland dress on all occasions, kept open house and was never seen without his 'tail', a body of armed retainers chosen from within the clan, who accompanied him everywhere. It is tempting to think of him as the last survivor of a noble breed, a chivalrous figure who kept to the old ways and was a father to his people. Unfortu- nately the reverse is true and proves that it was not only to the absentee landlords and the English speculators that the decay of the Highlands was due. Glengarry was one

93 A tribute to Queen Victoria's love of travelling and sketching in the Highlands; a sepia drawing signed 'Victoria Reg del. Ardverickie Sept: 1847'

94 Queen Victoria sketching at Loch Laggan, with the Prince of Wales and the Princess Royal, an engraving from the picture by Sir Edwin Landseer. It was the Queen's Christmas present to the Prince Consort in 1847

who wasted his substance, dispersed his clan and mortgaged his ancestral acres. At his death the son to whom he left nothing, having nothing to leave, was obliged to emigrate, and since then the Glengarry lands have passed out of the possession of the Macdonnells. The Raeburn portrait of the chief, one of the artist's finest pictures, shows him wearing a tartan that might be a combination of Glengarry

and old Stewart [figure 83]. It is certainly not the same as any of the modern Macdonald setts.

The appearance of James Logan's book in 1831 acted as a spur on every manufacturer in Scotland to produce new clan tartans in ever-increasing numbers for the clients who never ceased to demand them. Thomas Smibert might deplore the fact that 'the Highland chiefs themselves...

have been too ready to adopt changes at the mere dictation
of fancy with the view of improving, no doubt, the look
of their family setts', but once the fashion was launched
there was no going back on it. Smibert himself, and others
like him who had a genuine interest in the subject, did
their best to distinguish between what was old and what
was new, but their efforts were constantly frustrated by

95 An engraving from
Landseer's picture,
Queen Victoria landing
at Loch Muick, 1852.
She was the first
Sovereign of Great
Britain to have a house
in Scotland, at Balmoral

the inventive genius of the weavers and their clients. In
1850, one of the most famous of all the tartan manufactur-
ing firms, the brothers Smith of Mauchline, did succeed in
producing some order out of chaos, when they brought
out a book with the menacing title of *The Authenticated
Tartans of the Clans and Families of Scotland*. Forty years
later D. W. Stewart produced what is undoubtedly the

96 Various modern *skean dhus*; these are worn every day, tucked into the top of a stocking

97 A modern *skean dhu*. These small knives were first worn after the '45 when the wearing of dirks became illegal

most unusual of all tartan books, *Old and Rare Scottish Tartans*, in which the illustrations, forty-five in number, consist of actual squares of the tartans themselves, made from hand-woven silk. One enterprising weaver turned the success of the *Waverley* novels to good account by inventing a new sett, which he christened Meg Merrilees, in honour of the gipsy in *Guy Mannering*. A hundred years later the same tartan, its origin now entirely forgotten, was listed as a family tartan, under the name of Merrilees alone.

The Celtic revival owes much to Queen Victoria's devotion to the Highlands. 'At a quarter past seven o'clock', the Queen recorded in her *Journal of Our Life in the Highlands* in the autumn of 1855, 'we all arrived at Balmoral... the new house looks beautiful... an old shoe was thrown after us into the house for good luck when we entered the hall. The house is charming, the rooms delightful, the furniture, papers, everything perfection.' It was the first time that she had seen the castle since the new alterations had taken place and from the first she delighted in all she saw. 'This dear Paradise' is what it became to her then, and it remained so ever afterwards.

It was in 1842 that the Queen and Prince Albert had paid their first visit to Scotland. They were entertained for some days by Lord Breadalbane in Perthshire, and here for the first time they discovered the Highlands. To the Queen 'the *coup d'oeil* was indescribable' while the Prince Consort found it put him very much in mind of Switzerland. Five years later they were back, and this time, using the Royal Yacht, they explored all the west coast as far north as the Hebrides. It rained with monotonous persistance throughout the visit, and as a result of this, the half-formed plan to buy a house somewhere in the west Highlands was abandoned and instead the Queen's thoughts turned to Deeside, of which she had heard good reports. In 1848 Balmoral, a modern castle built round the nucleus of a much older house, was leased to the Royal family for the first time.

The property had belonged in Jacobite times to the Farquharsons, one of whom, 'Balmoral the Brave', had taken part in both the '15 and the '45. At an earlier date the Braes of Mar, lying a little to the west of Balmoral, were one of the favourite hunting grounds of the Scottish Kings, and when Queen Mary 'took the sport of hunting the deer in the forest of Mar and Atholl', it is recorded

98 Portrait of an unknown boy by Kenneth McKay, 1870, showing how children's clothes were adapted to wear with a kilt

99 HIGHLAND TARTANS

1 Macdonald of the Isles,
2 Cameron of Lochiel,
3 Dress Macleod,
4 Hunting Maclean,
5 Campbell of Argyll,
6 Royal Stewart
7 Hunting Fraser,
8 Robertson,
9 Mackenzie,
10 Mackintosh,
11 Mackay,
12 Rob Roy
13 Menzies,
14 Macfarlane,
15 MacDougall,
16 Grant,
17 Farquharson,
18 Hunting Chisholm

100 A page from Messrs Scott Adie's Catalogue in the 1890s, illustrating the latest fashionable dress for going shooting in Scotland

101 George Stirling Home Drummond at Abercairney, painted by J. M. Barclay in 1873, in everyday dress

that she and her party accounted for three hundred and fifty-six deer, five wolves and some roe. Although she enjoyed her visit to the Highlands, even declaring that it made her long to have been born a man, 'to know what life it was to lie all night in the fields, or to walk in the causeway with a jack and knapschalle (steel cap), a Glasgow buckler and a broad sword', Queen Mary showed no desire to live there permanently. Falkland and Holyrood were the palaces of sixteenth-century Scotland, and Linlithgow, where she herself was born. It was not until Queen Victoria came to live at Balmoral that any Scottish sovereign had entertained the notion of acquiring a permanent seat in the Highlands.

102 A plaid has many uses; from Messrs Scott Adie's Catalogue

103 An early photograph of the Princess of Wales (afterwards Queen Alexandra), taken at Mar Lodge at the time of the Braemar Gathering, probably in 1864

When the property became hers, four years after it had first been leased to the Royal family, a decision was made to replace the old buildings with something more in keeping with contemporary taste. The new castle was built to the design of a local architect, but as the Prince Consort's wishes were consulted at every step, to the Queen it was his creation, and his alone. When at last it was finished no-one could doubt that the Celtic revival had come to stay. Writing soon after to her sister, Lady Augusta Stanley, who was then Lady-in-Waiting to the Duchess of Kent, described in some detail the furnishings of the new house. 'The general wood-work is light coloured maple and birch chiefly, with locks and hinges silvered... Besides

83

104 A MacAlister in his clan tartan leaving Scotland for Canada at the time of the Clearances, which began to depopulate the Highlands at the end of the eighteenth century and continued well into the nineteenth

there are beautiful things, chandeliers of Parian, Highlanders, beautifully designed figures holding the light... appropriate trophies, and table ornaments in the same style.' The tartan motif was everywhere repeated. There were carpets in Royal Stewart as well as in the hunting sett. 'The curtains of the same Dress Stewart and a few chintz with a thistle pattern, the chairs and sofas in the

105 LOWLAND TARTANS

1 Grey Douglas,
2 Hamilton,
3 Lindsay
4 Kennedy,
5 Hay,
6 Bruce
7 Scott,
8 Graham of Montrose,
9 Ogilvy

REGIMENTAL AND RARE TARTANS

10 Lennox,
11 Johore,
12 Cameron of Erracht
13 Black Watch,
14 Murray of Atholl,
15 Gordon
16 Jacobite,
17 Clergy,
18 Lochaber

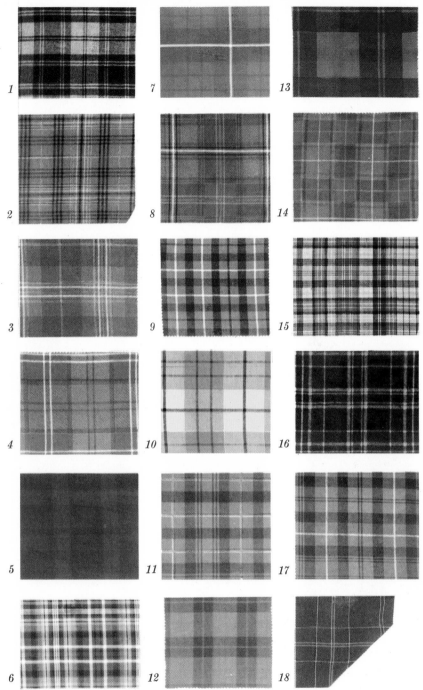

drawing-room Dress Stewart poplin. All highly character-istic, but not all equally *flatteuse* to the eye.' Even the draperies in the carriages were of Royal Stewart materi-al, and in addition to the old tartans two new ones were invented; the Victoria, which we owe to the Queen, and the better known Balmoral, of which the Prince Consort was the designer.

Once settled in Aberdeenshire, Queen Victoria allowed full rein to her interest in everything pertaining to Highland life [figure 94]. She had always enjoyed dancing, and at Balmoral everybody was encouraged to take part in the reels and country dances that she herself loved to see performed. Even in England the habit persisted, and when balls were given at Windsor or in London, it was not only mazurkhas and gavottes that were seen, but Scottish dances, whose unfamiliar patterns must have been a source of constant anxiety to the foreign diplomats. Dancing was not the only form of exercise the Queen favoured. One of the most surprising things about the Victorians was the pleasure they took in walking, and to this rule she was no exception. Moreover, she enjoyed every kind of expedition, and would travel over rough tracks and in all weathers with little or no regard for time or comfort [figure 95]. The distances covered seem by modern standards enormous—as much as sixty miles sometimes in a single day. Even allowing for the fact that ponies and carriages were used for the longer journeys, it must still have required considerable stamina to embark on them at all.

Ever since Queen Victoria died, a reaction of the most violent kind has set in against all that is represented by the dread word 'Balmorality'. For years comic ghillies, and even more comic lairds, kilts, whisky and Scottish Baronial architecture have provided material for innumerable jibes. Nor is it hard to see why this should be so. The Victorians, among other qualities, were possessed of an overwhelming desire to transform and improve almost everything on which they laid their hands. And as there was no lack of money in the latter half of the nineteenth century, this instinct was given full play. In Scotland the result, aesthetically speaking, was calamitous. A country that had always been very poor found itself suddenly rich, and at a time when ostentation was a sin very easily forgiven. What followed was an orgy of destruction affecting all branches of the arts, but architecture perhaps the most. We owe it to the Victorians that in the whole city of Glasgow there are now only five buildings more than three hundred years old, the Cathedral being one of them, while in Edinburgh the banality of Princes Street has to stand comparison with the inspiration of the Adam brothers on the one hand, and the roistering panache of the Old Town on the other The Highlands were partic-

106 The Edwardian traveller made himself very comfortable with his plaid and iron foot-warmer; from a Catalogue of Messrs Scott Adie

107 The Victorians
wore plain, unosten-
tatious Highland
everyday costume
and for shooting,
compared to the riot-
ous finery of their
evening dress

ularly vulnerable, as they were almost entirely un-developed, and obviously ripe for improvement. When it was known that the Queen had bought a property in the north, their popularity was assured. Although Balmoral has been blamed for all the excesses committed then and later in its name, the criticism is to a large extent un-justified. The pepper-pot castle, tartan carpets, and

108 Sir Edwin Landseer painted this picture of the seventh Duke of Atholl as a boy, with his ghillies, all wearing Murray of Atholl tartan

romantic attachment to Jacobitism, all these elements, it is true, were present at Balmoral, but there was every reason why they should be, as they were part of a fashion to which most of Scotland already subscribed. If Queen Victoria had never bought a house in the High-lands it would have done nothing to check the popularity of songs such as *The Bonny Bonny Banks of Loch Lomond* and there would still, without doubt, be tartan souvenirs in all the shops.

Tartans Today

109 A parade of Cameron Highlanders before Holyroodhouse, with the Regiment in full dress, painted by MacIan, c. 1870

IN ONE WAY THE Celtic revival conferred a benefit on Scotland, for in an age of violent change, it strengthened the feeling of continuity with the past. Without the great interest of the nineteenth century, tartan, for one thing, would probably have ceased to be worn altogether, and the fate of the traditional Highland trews would also have overtaken the kilt. As it is, tartan continues to be an acceptable form of modern dress, and such is the hold it has on the imagination that whenever some new use

89

110 A children's dancing competition at the Aboyne Games, in which the girls are wearing clothes identical to the boys. Recently this has been discouraged and the girls now wear white frocks and tartan sashes

is found for it, within a very short space of time this will have grown into a tradition, too sacred to touch. Tartan sashes are a case in point. Until the present century, it was unknown for the ladies at Highland balls to wear tartan, other than in the form of a dress, or a 'screen' (shawl) draped round the shoulders. Then of a sudden a new fashion prevailed and everyone who could lay claim to a tartan started to wear it in the form of a long sash, passed over the shoulder and secured with a brooch. To-day at all the Highland meetings, as the annual subscription balls at Inverness, Oban and in other places are called, nearly all the women wear them and it is an unwritten law that they must all be worn over the left shoulder, and never on the right [figure 115]. For men, the sartorial rules are less inflexible and it is no uncommon sight to see together on the same ballroom floor a dancer in the full panoply of the eighteenth century, with kilt and jacket in two different tartans; another wearing a

111 Modern sporting dress; from Messrs Scott Adie's Catalogue

112 Sir Ian Malcolm, seventeenth of Poltalloch, in Malcolm tartan, by Sir William Orpen

plain velvet doublet with lace jabot and cuffs; and a third exhibiting the most modern version of all, a short black coat and bow tie. Plaids, for evening use, are now virtually unknown, though they were once made in fine silk for great occasions. The Sobieski Stuarts claimed to have seen one at Cluny that had been especially woven in Spain for one of the chiefs. It was said of them, as it is of Kashmir shawls, that they could be pulled without difficulty through a wedding ring.

113 The Cameron Highlanders embarking at Gibraltar, wearing fatigue clothes, by MacIan

It has now become the fashion for dress tartans to be worn in the evening, while the hunting version of the sett is reserved for more humdrum occasions. While no one would wish to quarrel with this, it ought to be remembered that the distinction is of quite recent origin, and binding on no one. In any case, not all clans and families possess

114 A contemporary photograph showing a Black Watch Piper and two Privates, one of whom is wearing No. 1 or full-dress uniform. The piper is in Royal Stewart, the others wear the sett originally designed when the Regiment was first raised in 1742

two tartans. For everyday wear the kilt, whether it be made of dress or of hunting tartan, can boast of great practical advantages, without which, indeed, it would hardly have survived so long [figure 111]. It does not cling to the legs when wet, as trousers do, nor is it so hot for walking. And at all times the thick pleats at the back are a protection against both wind and rain. Women in kilts are not encouraged, perhaps rightly so, as it is not a garment calculated to flatter the female form. Until recently the girl dancers who competed at the various Highland games were allowed to dress in the same clothes as the boys, and it was a very melancholy spectacle to see such a jumble of buckles, tartan, velvet and cheap lace figure 110]. The organizers themselves now seem to have reached the same conclusion, and under the new rules it is no longer possible for competitors to appear looking like characters out of the pantomime.

One question about tartan alone remains to be answered, and it is the one most frequently asked; namely, who is entitled to wear it. Strictly speaking, only those whose families possess tartans of their own can claim historically that they have a right to assume them. But as this rule is broken by the vast majority of tartan users, and gives great offence to those who base their claims on a Scottish grandmother, there is no likelihood of its being generally accepted. Looking back on the history of tartan, it is

115 Dancing at a Highland Ball. The men are in kilts with short black jackets, others are in regimental uniforms

116 An Edwardian gentleman at a ball. Except for the height of the collar, modern evening dress is very similar; programmes are still used at Scottish subscription balls

117 A contemporary Highland child, dressed in comfortable everyday clothes. Portrait of the Hon. Andrew Fraser by H. Riddle

118 The Order of Release by Sir John Millais. This romantic impression of Highland military uniform is wrong in almost every detail: the kilt might be Gordon, the stockings belong to no known regiment

hard to explain how anything genuine could have survived the shoddy commercialization to which it has been subjected. And yet when all has been said, in spite of the vulgarity and the sticky sentiment, there still lurks, behind the garish shop window, a quality heroic and irrational, of which tartan is to some degree emblematic, and it is to this indefinable quality, the saving virtue of the Scottish race, that this book is dedicated.